BUILDING INTELLIGENT APPLICATION WITH PYTHON AND CLAUDE 3.5 SDK

LIAM HENRY JR

Table of Contents

Introduction: Unveiling the Secrets of Artificial Intelligence

Artificial intelligence (AI) is no longer a distant dream; it's woven into the fabric of our daily lives. This book will be your key to unlocking its potential, using Claude 3.5, a groundbreaking large language model (LLM), as a starting point.

Claude 3.5 showcases the remarkable feats AI can achieve, from tackling complex data analysis to sparking creative ideas and even collaborating on tasks. But this book goes beyond showcasing its features. We'll embark on a thrilling journey to explore the vast potential of AI and how it's transforming our world.

Whether you're a seasoned tech enthusiast or simply someone curious about the future, this book is designed to inform and engage you. Here's what awaits you:

Decoding Claude 3.5: We'll crack the code on Claude 3.5's practical applications, from automating tedious tasks to accelerating scientific breakthroughs and even fueling creative endeavors.

The Ethical Labyrinth: We'll navigate the complex ethical considerations surrounding AI development and deployment. Issues like bias, fairness, and human oversight will be critically examined to ensure AI serves humanity responsibly.

A Glimpse into Tomorrow: We'll cast a futuristic gaze on potential directions for AI, building upon the foundation laid by Claude 3.5. Specialization, human-AI partnerships, and the rise of AI companions are just a peek at the exciting possibilities that lie ahead.

AI for a Better World: We'll explore how AI can be harnessed to tackle global challenges in areas like climate change, healthcare, and education. The potential for AI to create a more sustainable and equitable future will be brought to light.

Building Responsible AI: We'll emphasize the importance of responsible development and human-centered design principles. Strategies for mitigating bias, ensuring transparency, and maintaining human control over AI systems will be discussed.

By the end of this book, you'll gain a deeper understanding of AI's potential, its current capabilities as exemplified by Claude 3.5, and the critical considerations for its future development and applications. Get ready to be an informed and engaged participant in the exciting age of AI. Let's begin our exploration!

Preface: Unveiling the Potential of AI with Claude 3.5 and Beyond

Artificial intelligence (AI) is rapidly transforming our world. From the way we interact with technology to the way we solve complex problems, AI's influence is undeniable. This book delves into the exciting potential of AI, using Claude 3.5, a powerful large language model (LLM), as a springboard for exploration.

Claude 3.5 showcases the remarkable capabilities of AI in automating tasks, generating creative text formats, and analyzing information. However, this book goes beyond simply exploring Claude 3.5's functionalities. We embark on a journey to envision the future of AI and its potential impact on various aspects of our lives.

This book is intended for a broad audience – anyone curious about AI and its potential. Whether you're a seasoned tech enthusiast or simply someone who wants to understand how AI might affect your daily life, this book offers valuable insights and thought-provoking discussions.

Here's a glimpse of what awaits you in the following chapters:

Unveiling Claude 3.5's Capabilities: We delve into the practical applications of Claude 3.5, exploring its potential to automate repetitive tasks, enhance scientific discovery, and augment creative processes.

The Ethical Landscape of AI: We address the crucial considerations and ethical implications surrounding AI development and deployment. Issues like bias, fairness, and human oversight are explored to ensure AI is used responsibly.

A Glimpse into the Future: We explore potential future directions for AI, building upon the foundation laid by Claude 3.5.

Specialization, human-AI collaboration, and the rise of AI companions are just some of the exciting possibilities on the horizon.

AI for Social Good: We examine how AI can be harnessed to address global challenges in areas like climate change, healthcare, and education. The potential for AI to contribute to a more sustainable and equitable future is explored.

Responsible AI Development: We emphasize the importance of responsible AI development and human-centered design principles. Strategies for mitigating bias, ensuring transparency, and maintaining human control over AI systems are discussed.

By the end of this book, you will have gained a deeper understanding of AI's potential, its current capabilities as exemplified by Claude 3.5, and the critical considerations for its responsible development and future applications. We stand at the precipice of a new era driven by AI, and this book equips you to be an informed and engaged participant in this exciting journey.

Let's begin!

Chapter 1: Introduction to Claude 3.5 Sonnet

This chapter dives into the world of Claude 3.5 Sonnet, a powerful large language model that is revolutionizing the field of artificial intelligence. We'll explore its core functionalities and understand how it can be leveraged to build intelligent applications.

1.1 What is Claude 3.5 Sonnet?

Claude 3.5 Sonnet is a cutting-edge large language model (LLM) developed by Anthropic AI. LLMs are a type of artificial intelligence (AI) trained on massive amounts of text data, enabling them to generate text, translate languages, write different kinds of creative content, and answer your questions in an informative way. Here's a deeper dive into what makes Claude 3.5 Sonnet special:

Powerhouse Performance: Claude 3.5 Sonnet stands out for its speed and efficiency. Compared to its predecessor, Claude 3 Opus, it boasts double the processing speed while maintaining accuracy.

Master of Many Trades: Claude 3.5 Sonnet isn't a one-trick pony. It excels in various tasks, including generating different creative text formats like poems or code, understanding and responding to complex prompts, and even translating languages.

Reasoning with the Best: Claude 3.5 Sonnet demonstrates impressive reasoning abilities, achieving top marks on benchmarks that assess graduate-level logical thinking. This makes it a valuable tool for tasks requiring analysis and problem-solving.

In short, Claude 3.5 Sonnet is a powerful and versatile LLM that can be a game-changer for various applications. It brings speed, accuracy, and strong reasoning capabilities to the table, making it a leader in the field of AI.

1.2 Key Features and Capabilities

Claude 3.5 Sonnet packs a punch with a variety of impressive features that make it a versatile tool for building intelligent applications. Here's a closer look at some of its key strengths:

Advanced Text Generation: Claude 3.5 Sonnet goes beyond simple text creation. It can craft various creative text formats, like poems, code, scripts, musical pieces, emails, letters, etc. You can provide it with a starting prompt or idea, and it will use its knowledge to generate original and coherent content.

Code Manipulation Mastery: Claude 3.5 Sonnet is a programmer's dream come true. It can assist with tasks like code completion, fixing errors, and even translating code from one language to another. This significantly improves developer productivity and helps maintain clean, efficient code.

Reasoning Powerhouse: Claude 3.5 Sonnet isn't just about generating text; it can also think critically. It consistently ranks high on benchmarks that assess logical reasoning abilities, making it a valuable asset for tasks that require analysis, problem-solving, and coming to well-supported conclusions based on information.

State-of-the-Art Vision: Claude 3.5 Sonnet surpasses its predecessors in visual understanding. It excels at interpreting charts, graphs, and complex diagrams, making it a powerful tool for data analysis and visualization. Additionally, it can accurately transcribe text from imperfect images, a feature with significant applications in various industries.

Enhanced Information Management with Artifacts: A new feature in Claude 3.5 Sonnet is Artifacts. This allows you to store and reference important information during conversations with the model. This improves the coherence and flow of interactions, especially when dealing with complex topics or multi-step tasks.

These are just some of the key features that make Claude 3.5 Sonnet a standout LLM. Its capabilities empower developers to build intelligent applications that can handle complex tasks, generate creative text formats, and solve problems with exceptional reasoning abilities.

1.3 Advantages over Other Language Models

Claude 3.5 Sonnet boasts several advantages over other large language models, making it a compelling choice for various applications. Here's a breakdown of its key strengths:

Efficiency Edge: Claude 3.5 Sonnet delivers exceptional performance at a competitive price. Compared to its predecessors, it offers double the processing speed while maintaining accuracy. This translates to faster development cycles and cost-effective AI solutions.

Superior Reasoning: Claude 3.5 Sonnet shines in its ability to reason logically. It consistently outperforms other models on benchmarks designed to test graduate-level critical thinking. This makes it ideal for tasks requiring complex analysis, problem-solving, and drawing well-founded conclusions based on evidence.

Focus on Safety and Trust: Claude 3.5 Sonnet prioritizes safety and trustworthiness. Anthropic, the developers behind Claude, have implemented safeguards to minimize the generation of misleading or harmful content. This is crucial for applications where accuracy and reliability are paramount, such as in healthcare, finance, and legal domains.

Context Champion: Claude 3.5 Sonnet excels at understanding and maintaining context over long stretches of text. Its impressive

200,000 token context window allows it to remember and reference information from earlier parts of a conversation, leading to more coherent and relevant interactions, especially beneficial for applications requiring ongoing dialogues or multi-step workflows.

Multilingual Mastery: While many LLMs offer multilingual capabilities, Claude 3.5 Sonnet stands out for its exceptional performance in translation tasks. It can translate between languages accurately while preserving the meaning and nuances of the original text.

These advantages make Claude 3.5 Sonnet a strong contender in the LLM landscape. Its speed, efficiency, superior reasoning abilities, focus on safety, and exceptional context management make it a versatile tool for developers building intelligent applications in various fields.

Chapter 2: Understanding the Power of Python

Python is the language of choice for unlocking the potential of Claude 3.5 Sonnet and building intelligent applications. This chapter explores why Python is such a perfect fit and equips you with the foundational knowledge to get started.

2.1 Why Python for Claude 3.5 Sonnet Applications?

There are several compelling reasons why Python is the perfect partner for building intelligent applications with Claude 3.5 Sonnet. Here's a closer look at the key advantages:

Beginner-Friendly: Python's syntax is known for its readability and resemblance to plain English. This makes it much easier to learn and write code, even for those with no prior programming experience. Unlike some other languages with complex syntax, Python allows you to focus on the logic and functionality of your application rather than getting bogged down in intricate details. This is especially beneficial when working with complex AI concepts like Claude 3.5 Sonnet.

AI and Machine Learning Powerhouse: The Python ecosystem thrives on a vast collection of libraries and frameworks specifically designed for AI and machine learning tasks. Popular options like TensorFlow, Keras, and Scikit-learn provide pre-built functions and tools that streamline development. These libraries handle complex computations and algorithms under the hood, allowing you to focus on integrating Claude 3.5 Sonnet's functionalities into your application with ease. Additionally, libraries like the Claude 3.5 SDK simplify interaction with the model's capabilities.

Versatility Across the Board: Python's strength lies in its ability to handle various aspects of application development. From data manipulation and analysis to building user interfaces, Python provides the tools you need. This versatility is crucial for building intelligent applications that interact with data, make decisions based on Claude 3.5 Sonnet's outputs, and present information to users in a clear and intuitive way. As your applications grow in complexity, Python scales seamlessly to accommodate your evolving needs.

Thriving Community Support: The global Python community is massive and active, with a wealth of developers, researchers, and enthusiasts. This translates to readily available online resources, tutorials, and forums for troubleshooting and learning. Whether you encounter a specific challenge while working with Claude 3.5 Sonnet or simply need guidance on best practices, there's a strong support network available to help you on your journey.

2.2 Essential Python Concepts for AI Development

Building intelligent applications with Claude 3.5 Sonnet requires a solid foundation in Python. This section dives into the core concepts you'll need to master to effectively interact with the model and manipulate data.

Variables and Data Types:

Variables act as containers that store data used by your program. You'll learn how to declare variables with meaningful names and assign different data types to them. These data types define the kind of information a variable can hold, such as integers (whole numbers), floats (decimal numbers), strings (text), and booleans (True or False).

Mastering how to perform basic operations like addition, subtraction, multiplication, and division on these data types is essential for manipulating the information used by your AI application.

Control Flow Statements:

These statements dictate the execution flow of your program. They allow you to make decisions and repeat tasks based on specific conditions.

Conditional statements (if/else) are crucial for building intelligent applications that can react differently based on Claude 3.5 Sonnet's outputs. For example, an if statement could check the sentiment of text generated by Claude 3.5 Sonnet and adjust the application's response accordingly.

Loops (for/while) enable you to repeat a block of code a specific number of times or until a certain condition is met. This is essential for tasks like iterating through data sets or repeatedly sending prompts to Claude 3.5 Sonnet and processing the results.

Functions:

Functions are reusable blocks of code that perform specific tasks. They promote code modularity and reusability, making your programs more organized and easier to maintain. When working with Claude 3.5 Sonnet, you can define functions to handle repetitive tasks, such as pre-processing prompts before sending them to the model or formatting the outputs for user display.

Data Structures:

Python offers built-in data structures like lists, dictionaries, and tuples that allow you to organize and manage complex data efficiently. These structures are essential for storing and manipulating the information used by your AI applications:

Lists are ordered collections of items, useful for storing sequences of data like prompts, outputs from Claude 3.5 Sonnet, or intermediate results during processing.

Dictionaries store data as key-value pairs, making them ideal for situations where you need to associate information with specific labels. For example, you could use a dictionary to store different configurations for interacting with Claude 3.5 Sonnet.

Tuples are immutable ordered collections, meaning their contents cannot be changed after creation. They are useful for situations where you need to represent fixed data sets.

By grasping these fundamental Python concepts, you'll be well-equipped to build the foundation for your intelligent applications. The next section will guide you through setting up your development environment and writing your first Python program to solidify your understanding.

2.3 Setting Up Your Python Development Environment

Now that you understand the benefits of Python for Claude 3.5 Sonnet applications and the core concepts you'll need, it's time to set up your development environment. This section will equip you with the tools you need to start coding.

2.3.1 Choosing Your Tools

Here's an overview of the essential tools for your Python development journey:

Python Interpreter: This is the core program that executes Python code. The most popular option is CPython, the reference implementation of Python. You can download it for free from the official Python website (https://www.python.org/downloads/).

Integrated Development Environment (IDE): An IDE provides a comprehensive environment for writing, editing, debugging, and running Python code. Popular options include PyCharm, Visual Studio Code, and Spyder. These IDEs offer features like code completion, syntax highlighting, and debugging tools to streamline your development process.

AI and Machine Learning Libraries: As mentioned earlier, Python boasts a rich ecosystem of libraries specifically designed for AI and machine learning tasks. Here are some key ones for working with Claude 3.5 Sonnet:

TensorFlow: A powerful open-source library for numerical computation and deep learning.

Keras: A high-level API built on top of TensorFlow, known for its user-friendly approach to building and training neural networks.

Scikit-learn: A comprehensive library for machine learning tasks like classification, regression, and clustering. While Scikit-learn might not be directly used for interacting with Claude 3.5 Sonnet, it provides valuable tools for data manipulation and pre-processing, which are often crucial steps in AI workflows.

Claude 3.5 SDK (Software Development Kit): This official library from Anthropic provides functions and classes specifically designed for interacting with Claude 3.5 Sonnet. It simplifies tasks like sending prompts, receiving outputs, and managing configurations.

2.3.2 Installation and Configuration

The installation process for Python and its libraries will vary slightly depending on your operating system (Windows, macOS, or Linux). Here are some general guidelines:

Installing Python: Refer to the official Python website (https://www.python.org/downloads/) for clear instructions on downloading and installing Python for your specific operating system. Most installations include the pip package manager, which you'll use to install additional libraries.

Installing Libraries: Once you have Python set up, you can use pip to install the libraries mentioned in the previous section. Open a terminal or command prompt and run commands like `pip install tensorflow` or `pip install keras`. The Claude 3.5 SDK installation instructions will likely be available on Anthropic's website or documentation.

2.3.3 Writing Your First Python Program

Let's solidify your understanding with a simple Python program. Here's an example that prints "Hello, world!":

Python

```
print("Hello, world!")
```

Save this code in a file named `hello_world.py` and run it from your terminal using the command `python hello_world.py`. If everything is set up correctly, you should see "Hello, world!" printed on your screen.

This is a basic example, but it demonstrates how to write and execute Python code. As you progress through this book, you'll build upon these fundamentals to create more complex and intelligent applications with Claude 3.5 Sonnet.

Additional Tips:

Consult the official documentation for Python (https://docs.python.org/) and the libraries you choose to install. They provide detailed information on usage, tutorials, and best practices.

Online communities and forums are valuable resources for troubleshooting and learning. Don't hesitate to seek help if you encounter challenges during the setup process.

By setting up your development environment and practicing with basic Python code, you'll be well-prepared to delve into the exciting world of building intelligent applications with Claude 3.5 Sonnet.

Chapter 3: Demystifying the Claude 3.5 SDK

The Claude 3.5 SDK acts as the bridge between your Python code and the powerful capabilities of Claude 3.5 Sonnet. This chapter unveils the functionalities of the SDK, equipping you to interact with the model and harness its potential.

3.1 Installation and Configuration

Equipping your Python environment with the Claude 3.5 SDK is the first step to unlocking the power of Claude 3.5 Sonnet in your applications. This section will guide you through the installation process and configuration steps.

Obtaining the SDK

There are two main ways to acquire the Claude 3.5 SDK:

Direct Download: Anthropic, the developers of Claude 3.5 Sonnet, likely provides the SDK for download on their website. Look for a downloads section or specific instructions for developers. This might involve downloading a compressed file (like a zip archive) containing the SDK files.

Package Manager: If Anthropic distributes the SDK through a package manager like pip, you can install it directly from your terminal or command prompt using a command like `pip install claude35-sdk`. This approach is convenient as it handles dependency management, ensuring you have all the necessary libraries for the SDK to function correctly.

Refer to Official Documentation:

For the most up-to-date and accurate information, it's crucial to consult Anthropic's official documentation for the Claude 3.5 SDK. Here are some resources you might find helpful:

Anthropic Website: Look for a developer section or specific documentation related to Claude 3.5 Sonnet and its SDK. Anthropic might provide a dedicated webpage with download links, installation instructions, and usage examples.

SDK Documentation: The downloaded SDK package might come with its own documentation. This documentation should detail the installation process, configuration steps, available functions and classes, and code examples to get you started.

General Installation Steps (assuming a downloadable archive):

Download the SDK: Head to Anthropic's website and locate the download section for the Claude 3.5 SDK. Download the appropriate file for your operating system (Windows, macOS, or Linux).

Extract the Archive: Once downloaded, extract the compressed file (e.g., .zip or .tar.gz) to a suitable location on your computer. This will typically create a folder containing the SDK files.

Set Up Environment Variables (Optional): Some SDKs might require setting environment variables to specify the location of the SDK files. Refer to the official documentation for specific instructions on this step.

Configuration and Authentication

Once you have the SDK installed, you'll need to configure it to connect to Claude 3.5 Sonnet. This typically involves providing your authentication credentials.

API Key or Access Token: Anthropic likely provides a mechanism to obtain an API key or access token for your Claude

3.5 account. This key acts as your unique identifier and grants authorized access to the model. You'll typically find instructions for obtaining these credentials on Anthropic's developer dashboard.

SDK Configuration: The SDK will provide a way to configure it with your API key or access token. This might involve setting a configuration variable within your Python code or potentially creating a configuration file. The specific instructions will depend on the chosen installation method (downloaded archive or pip) and the SDK's design.

By following these steps and consulting Anthropic's documentation, you'll successfully install and configure the Claude 3.5 SDK, preparing you to interact with Claude 3.5 Sonnet from your Python applications. The next sections will explore the core functionalities and potential advanced features the SDK offers.

3.2 Core Components and Functionalities of the SDK

The Claude 3.5 SDK acts as a bridge between your Python code and the powerful capabilities of Claude 3.5 Sonnet. By leveraging the SDK's functionalities, you can seamlessly send prompts to the model, receive its responses, and manage the interaction effectively. Here's a breakdown of the SDK's core components:

Model Selection:

Claude 3.5 Sonnet might offer different model variants with varying capabilities or specializations. For instance, there could be a model optimized for code generation or another fine-tuned for scientific tasks.

The SDK provides a mechanism to select the appropriate model for your application's needs. This might involve specifying a model name or identifier within your Python code when interacting with the SDK.

Prompt Crafting and Input Management:

Crafting well-defined prompts is essential for guiding Claude 3.5 Sonnet towards the desired outcome. The SDK offers functionalities to assist you in constructing effective prompts:

Text formatting options to enhance clarity and structure.

Specifying creative text formats (like poems, code, scripts) to tailor the output.

The ability to incorporate data or instructions relevant to your task.

Depending on Claude 3.5 Sonnet's capabilities, the SDK might also allow for handling different input modalities beyond just text, such as images or audio.

Sending Requests and Receiving Responses:

The SDK provides methods for sending your crafted prompts to Claude 3.5 Sonnet. This involves:

Packaging your prompt and potentially any additional data into the appropriate format.

Sending the request to Anthropic's servers using the SDK's communication functionalities.

The SDK handles communication behind the scenes and retrieves the model's generated responses. These responses can vary depending on your prompt and the model's capabilities. They could be:

Text in various formats (e.g., summaries, poems, code)

Translations between languages

Different creative text formats based on your specifications

Error Handling and Debugging:

Even with well-crafted prompts, errors or unexpected issues can occur during communication with Claude 3.5 Sonnet. The SDK should include mechanisms for handling these situations:

Providing informative error messages that pinpoint the issue's location within your code or prompt.

Offering debugging tools to help you identify and rectify errors in your prompts or code. This might involve utilities for logging communication details or inspecting the format of your requests.

By understanding these core functionalities, you'll be equipped to interact with Claude 3.5 Sonnet effectively from your Python applications. The next section will explore some advanced features that certain SDKs might offer for more specialized use cases.

3.3 Advanced Features (Optional)

While the core functionalities of the Claude 3.5 SDK provide a solid foundation for interacting with the model, some advanced SDKs might offer additional features to cater to specific use cases.

Here's a glimpse into some potential enhancements you might encounter:

Fine-Tuning and Customization:

Advanced SDKs might allow you to fine-tune Claude 3.5 Sonnet on your own datasets or tasks relevant to your application. This fine-tuning process involves training the model on your specific data to potentially improve its performance and tailor its responses to your domain. The SDK would likely provide functionalities for uploading your data, specifying fine-tuning parameters, and deploying the fine-tuned model for use within your application.

Batch Processing and Performance Optimization:

For applications that require sending numerous prompts or handling large datasets, the SDK might offer functionalities for batch processing. This involves grouping multiple prompts together and sending them to Claude 3.5 Sonnet as a batch, potentially improving efficiency compared to sending them individually. The SDK might also provide optimization techniques to streamline communication with Claude 3.5 Sonnet and reduce processing time.

Artifact Management (if applicable):

Claude 3.5 Sonnet might introduce a feature called Artifacts. These artifacts allow you to store and reference important information during conversations with the model. This can be particularly beneficial for complex tasks or multi-step workflows where maintaining context is crucial. An advanced SDK would provide tools for managing artifacts within your Python code. You could define, store, and reference these artifacts during interactions with Claude 3.5 Sonnet, ensuring a more coherent and consistent flow of information.

It's important to note that these advanced features may not be available in all SDKs. The specific capabilities will depend on the design choices made by Anthropic and the intended use cases for the SDK. Always refer to the official documentation for the Claude 3.5 SDK you're using to determine the exact features and functionalities it offers.

By understanding both the core functionalities and these potential advanced features, you'll be well-equipped to leverage the full potential of the Claude 3.5 SDK in your Python applications. The following chapters will delve into specific examples of how you can utilize the Claude 3.5 SDK to build intelligent applications.

Chapter 4: Text Generation and Manipulation with Claude 3.5

One of Claude 3.5 Sonnet's strengths lies in its ability to generate and manipulate text in various creative formats. This chapter explores how to leverage the Claude 3.5 SDK to unlock this potential and build intelligent applications.

4.1 Crafting Effective Prompts for Text Generation

When it comes to unlocking the potential of Claude 3.5 Sonnet for text generation, the magic lies in crafting effective prompts. These prompts act as instructions, guiding Claude 3.5 towards the kind of creative text output you desire. Here are some key principles to consider for writing effective prompts:

Clearly Defined Objective: Before diving into specifics, take a step back and identify the overarching goal. What kind of text do you want Claude 3.5 Sonnet to generate? Is it a poem, a news article summary, a code snippet, a captivating story, or something else entirely? Having a clear objective in mind sets the stage for crafting a focused and successful prompt.

Context is King: Claude 3.5 Sonnet thrives on context. Provide enough background information to establish the setting, introduce characters, or outline the overall theme. The more context you offer, the better Claude 3.5 can understand the nuances of your request and generate text that aligns with your vision.

Specificity is Key: Avoid vague or ambiguous language in your prompts. Instead, use precise keywords and descriptions to steer Claude 3.5 in the desired direction. For instance, instead of saying "write a story," you could provide a specific genre (science fiction, mystery) or starting prompt (A lone astronaut wakes up on a deserted spaceship).

Leverage Examples: If possible, include relevant examples in your prompts to illustrate the style or tone you're aiming for. This can be particularly helpful for creative text formats like poems or scripts. You could provide Claude 3.5 with a few lines of a poem in your preferred style or reference a famous movie with a similar tone for your script.

Instructional Power: Don't be afraid to provide instructions within your prompt. You can specify the desired length of the output, the narrative point of view (first person, third person), or even the emotional tone (humorous, suspenseful). The more specific you are, the more control you have over the generated text.

By following these guidelines and tailoring them to your specific use case, you'll be well on your way to crafting effective prompts that unlock the full potential of Claude 3.5 Sonnet's text generation capabilities. The next section will delve into how you can leverage these techniques to generate different creative text formats.

4.2 Generating Different Creative Text Formats

Claude 3.5 Sonnet's versatility extends beyond basic text generation. By incorporating the Claude 3.5 SDK and crafting effective prompts, you can unleash its creativity to produce various artistic text formats. Here's how to leverage the SDK for specific creative tasks:

Enchanting Poems:

Spark Claude 3.5 Sonnet's poetic abilities by providing a starting theme, rhyme scheme, or desired style (haiku, sonnet, limerick).

For instance, a prompt like "Write a sonnet about a robot who falls in love with a human" provides context, form (sonnet), and a touch of narrative direction.

Code Generation for Developers:

Enhance your development workflow by using Claude 3.5 Sonnet to generate code snippets.

Craft prompts that describe the functionality or problem you want the code to solve. Be specific about the programming language and desired algorithms.

An example prompt could be "Write a Python function to calculate the factorial of a number using recursion."

Captivating Scripts:

Breathe life into your story ideas by employing Claude 3.5 Sonnet to generate scripts.

Outline the plot, characters, and setting within your prompt. You can even specify the genre (comedy, thriller) or target audience (children, adults).

A prompt like "Write a movie script about a group of explorers who discover a lost civilization in the Amazon rainforest" provides a clear starting point for Claude 3.5 Sonnet.

Musical Compositions:

Claude 3.5 Sonnet can even assist with musical endeavors.

Craft prompts that describe the desired genre, mood (upbeat, melancholic), or specific instruments you have in mind.

While Claude 3.5 might not directly generate playable music, the output score can serve as a creative springboard for composers. A prompt like "Write a musical piece in the style of Tchaikovsky for a solo piano, filled with a sense of longing" sparks Claude 3.5's musical creativity.

Remember, the Claude 3.5 SDK often provides a way to specify the desired format within your prompt or function call (e.g., format="HAIKU" or format="PYTHON_FUNCTION"). Refer to the SDK's documentation for specific details on how to indicate the target creative text format.

By combining these techniques with your imagination, you can unlock new avenues for creative expression and enhance your projects with unique text formats generated by Claude 3.5 Sonnet. The next section will showcase illustrative code snippets to provide a clearer picture of how you might interact with the SDK for various text generation tasks.

4.3 Prompt Examples and Code Snippets (Illustrative Purposes Only)

While we can't access the exact inner workings of the Claude 3.5 SDK, here are some illustrative code snippets that demonstrate how you might interact with the SDK for different text generation tasks. These examples assume the SDK uses a `generate_text` function and allows specifying the desired format within the function call.

Generating a Poem

Python

```
# Generate a haiku about nature
poem_prompt = "Write a haiku poem about the
beauty of a sunrise."
```

```
poem_response                        =
sdk.generate_text(prompt=poem_prompt,
format="HAIKU")

print(poem_response)
```

This code snippet defines a prompt requesting a haiku poem about a sunrise. It then calls the `generate_text` function from the SDK, passing the prompt and specifying the desired format as "HAIKU". The output (poem_response) will contain the haiku generated by Claude 3.5 Sonnet.

Generating Python Code

Python

```
# Generate a Python function to sort a list of
numbers
code_prompt = "Write a Python function that takes
a list of numbers and returns a new list with the
numbers sorted in ascending order."
code_response                        =
sdk.generate_text(prompt=code_prompt,
format="PYTHON_FUNCTION")

print(code_response)
```

This example demonstrates generating Python code. The prompt clearly defines the function's purpose and includes comments for readability (although comments might not be part of the actual SDK call). The `format` argument specifies "PYTHON_FUNCTION" to indicate the desired output.

Important Note:

Remember that these are illustrative examples, and the actual syntax for the Claude 3.5 SDK might differ. Always refer to the official documentation for the specific SDK you're using to ensure you're using the correct function calls and formatting options.

The next section will explore how Claude 3.5 Sonnet can be utilized for text manipulation and summarization tasks.

4.4 Text Manipulation and Summarization

Claude 3.5 Sonnet's capabilities extend beyond crafting creative text formats from scratch. It can also be a valuable tool for manipulating and summarizing existing text, offering exciting possibilities for various applications. Here are some ways to leverage Claude 3.5 Sonnet for these tasks:

Concise Summarization: Information overload is a real problem in today's world. Claude 3.5 Sonnet can assist by generating summaries of lengthy articles, documents, or even research papers. Provide the text you want summarized as input, and Claude 3.5 Sonnet will produce a concise version that captures the main points.

Text Editing and Style Transfer: Imagine being able to effortlessly modify the tone, formality, or style of a piece of text. Claude 3.5 Sonnet makes this possible. Craft prompts that instruct the model on how to alter the text. You can adjust the formality (casual to professional), change the tone (humorous to serious), or even translate it to another language.

Creative Rewriting and Content Paraphrasing: Overcome writer's block or generate fresh perspectives on existing content. Provide Claude 3.5 Sonnet with a piece of text and instruct it to rewrite it in a different style, paraphrase the content while preserving meaning, or even expand on certain ideas to create new content.

Here's a breakdown of how these functionalities might translate into code (assuming the SDK uses a `generate_text` function with additional parameters for specifying the manipulation task):

Python

```python
# Summarize a news article
news_article = "This is a long news article..."
# Replace with actual article text
summary_response                          =
sdk.generate_text(text=news_article,
task="SUMMARIZE")

# Change the tone of a paragraph to humorous
paragraph = "This is a serious paragraph."
humorous_response                         =
sdk.generate_text(text=paragraph,
task="CHANGE_TONE", tone="HUMOROUS")

# Rewrite a sentence in a different style
sentence = "The cat sat on the mat."
rewrite_response                          =
sdk.generate_text(text=sentence, task="REWRITE")
```

These are just a few examples, and the possibilities are vast. By combining text manipulation techniques with Claude 3.5 Sonnet, you can automate tasks, enhance communication clarity, and even generate new creative content based on existing information.

Remember, the specific functionalities and available options for text manipulation might vary depending on the Claude 3.5 SDK you're using. Consult the SDK's documentation for a comprehensive overview of its capabilities.

The following chapter will delve into how Claude 3.5 Sonnet can empower you in the realm of code development.

Chapter 5: Unlocking the Potential of Claude 3.5 for Code Development

As a developer, you know the value of efficiency and tackling repetitive tasks. Claude 3.5 Sonnet steps in as a powerful companion, augmenting your development workflow in various ways. This chapter explores how to leverage Claude 3.5 for code development tasks.

5.1 Automating Repetitive Coding Tasks

As a developer, you know the feeling of spending too much time on mundane coding tasks. Claude 3.5 Sonnet can be a valuable asset in your workflow by automating repetitive coding tasks and freeing you to focus on more complex aspects of your projects. Here's how you can leverage Claude 3.5 Sonnet's capabilities in this area:

Code Generation:

Claude 3.5 Sonnet shines in its ability to generate code snippets in various programming languages. Here's how to leverage this for automation: * Identify repetitive code blocks that you frequently write. These can be common utility functions, data processing routines, or boilerplate code for specific tasks. * Craft clear and concise prompts that describe the desired functionality of the code you want to generate. The more specific you are, the better Claude 3.5 Sonnet can understand your intent and generate relevant code. * Integrate Claude 3.5 Sonnet's code generation into your development process. This could involve using the SDK from within your development environment or creating custom scripts to automate code generation for specific tasks.

Test Case Creation:

Writing comprehensive test cases is essential for robust code, but it can also be time-consuming. Claude 3.5 Sonnet can assist in automating test case creation: * Provide Claude 3.5 Sonnet with your existing code or a description of the functionality you want to test. * The SDK might offer a specific task argument (e.g., task="TEST_CASE") to indicate you want test cases generated. * Claude 3.5 Sonnet can then generate test cases that cover various scenarios, including edge cases you might not have considered, improving your code's overall quality.

By automating these repetitive tasks, you can significantly improve your development efficiency. Claude 3.5 Sonnet takes care of the mundane aspects, allowing you to focus on the creative problem-solving and strategic coding tasks that require human expertise.

The next section dives into how Claude 3.5 Sonnet can aid you in improving your code and tackling debugging challenges.

5.2 Code Improvement and Debugging

While Claude 3.5 Sonnet isn't a magic solution for all your debugging woes, it can be a valuable asset in your development toolbox. Here's how you can leverage Claude 3.5 Sonnet for code improvement and debugging:

Code Completion:

Writer's block can strike even in the coding world. Claude 3.5 Sonnet can assist you in overcoming roadblocks and expediting development by suggesting code completions: * As you write code, Claude 3.5 Sonnet can analyze the context and suggest relevant code snippets to complete functions, variable declarations, or control flow statements. * The SDK might offer a functionality like code completion that you can trigger within your development environment. * Remember to review and adapt these suggestions to ensure they align with your coding style and project requirements.

Bug Detection and Debugging Assistance:

Claude 3.5 Sonnet might not pinpoint bugs directly, but it can offer valuable insights to aid in the debugging process: * Describe the functionality of your code and the errors you're encountering. Provide Claude 3.5 Sonnet with relevant code snippets or error messages. * Claude 3.5 Sonnet might analyze your code and suggest potential issues or areas for inspection. It could highlight logical inconsistencies, potential syntax errors, or inefficiencies in your code's structure. * By leveraging these insights, you can narrow down the root cause of the bug and resolve it more effectively.

Here are some additional points to consider when using Claude 3.5 Sonnet for debugging:

Clarity is Key: The more precise you are in describing the issue and providing context to Claude 3.5 Sonnet, the more helpful its suggestions will be.

Human Expertise Remains Crucial: Claude 3.5 Sonnet is a powerful tool, but it shouldn't replace your own debugging expertise. Use your judgment and understanding of the code to interpret Claude 3.5 Sonnet's suggestions and identify the root cause of the bug.

Integration with Debuggers: While not yet a common feature, future iterations of Claude 3.5 Sonnet or the SDK might integrate with debuggers, allowing you to seamlessly interact with Claude 3.5 Sonnet's insights within your debugging workflow.

By combining Claude 3.5 Sonnet's capabilities with your problem-solving skills, you can streamline the debugging process and enhance the overall quality of your code. The next section will delve into how the Claude 3.5 SDK facilitates interaction with the model specifically for code development tasks.

5.3 Leveraging the Claude 3.5 SDK for Code Development

The Claude 3.5 SDK acts as a bridge between you and the powerful functionalities of Claude 3.5 Sonnet within the context of code development. Here's how the SDK can empower you:

Specifying Programming Language:

The SDK likely provides a way to indicate the desired programming language for the generated code. This ensures Claude 3.5 Sonnet adheres to the syntax and conventions of the chosen language (e.g., Python, Java, C++).

When crafting prompts or using functions for code generation, you might specify the language argument to guide Claude 3.5 Sonnet in its output.

Integration with Development Environments (IDEs):

Advanced SDKs might offer seamless integration with popular IDEs like Visual Studio Code or PyCharm. This integration can significantly enhance your workflow:

Imagine directly interacting with Claude 3.5 Sonnet from within your IDE. You could write prompts, generate code, and test functionalities without switching between different applications.

The SDK might provide functionalities like code completion suggestions powered by Claude 3.5 Sonnet, tailored to the context of your current code within the IDE.

Additional Code-Specific Functionalities:

The Claude 3.5 SDK might offer functionalities specifically designed for code development tasks beyond what's covered in previous sections. Here are some potential examples:

Code Formatting: Claude 3.5 Sonnet, guided by the SDK, could reformat your code according to specific style guides or coding conventions.

Code Comment Generation: The SDK might allow you to generate comments to explain the functionality of specific code sections, improving code readability and maintainability.

Remember: Refer to the official documentation for the specific Claude 3.5 SDK you're using to get a comprehensive understanding of its features and functionalities. The exact way to interact with the SDK and the available options might vary depending on the implementation.

The next section provides illustrative code snippets to showcase how you might interact with the SDK for code-related tasks. However, keep in mind that these are examples, and the actual syntax will depend on the specific SDK.

5.4 Code Examples and Prompt Crafting (Illustrative Purposes Only)

While we can't access the inner workings of specific Claude 3.5 SDKs, here are some illustrative code snippets that demonstrate how you might interact with the SDK for code-related tasks. These examples assume the SDK uses functions like `generate_code` and allows specifying the programming language and task (if applicable).

Generating Python Code

Python

```python
# Generate a Python function to reverse a string
code_prompt = "Write a Python function that takes
a string as input and returns the reversed
string."
code_response                                      =
sdk.generate_code(prompt=code_prompt,
language="PYTHON")

print(code_response)
```

This code snippet defines a prompt requesting a Python function to reverse a string. It then calls the generate_code function from the SDK, passing the prompt and specifying the language as "PYTHON". The output (code_response) will contain the Python code generated by Claude 3.5 Sonnet.

Generating Unit Tests (Python Example)

Python

```python
# Assume a function named sort_numbers exists
(function definition not shown)
test_prompt    =    "Write    unit    tests    for    the
sort_numbers function that ensure it sorts a list
of numbers in ascending order."
test_response                                      =
sdk.generate_code(prompt=test_prompt,
language="PYTHON", task="TEST_CASE")

print(test_response)
```

This example demonstrates generating unit tests for a sorting function. The prompt clearly defines the purpose of the test cases. The `language` argument specifies Python, and the `task` argument is set to "TEST_CASE" to indicate the desired functionality.

Important Note:

Remember that these are illustrative examples, and the actual syntax for the Claude 3.5 SDK might differ. Always refer to the official documentation for the specific SDK you're using to ensure you're using the correct function calls and formatting options.

Cautions and Best Practices

Review and Test Generated Code: The generated code snippets from Claude 3.5 Sonnet should always be reviewed and potentially modified before integrating them into your production codebase. It's essential to ensure the code adheres to your coding standards, functions as intended within your specific application context, and passes necessary security checks.

Start Simple and Iterate: Begin with well-defined prompts and tasks for Claude 3.5 Sonnet. As you gain experience and confidence, gradually introduce more complex coding challenges.

Human Expertise is Irreplaceable: Claude 3.5 Sonnet is a powerful tool that can augment your development capabilities, but it shouldn't replace your problem-solving skills and understanding of coding best practices.

By effectively utilizing Claude 3.5 Sonnet and its SDK, you can streamline your development workflow, enhance code quality, and potentially unlock new avenues for creative problem-solving in your projects. The following chapter will conclude this guide by exploring some general considerations and best practices for using Claude 3.5 Sonnet effectively.

Chapter 6: Building Chatbots and Conversational Interfaces with Claude 3.5

Claude 3.5's text generation and manipulation capabilities open exciting possibilities for crafting interactive chatbots and conversational interfaces. This chapter explores how to leverage Claude 3.5 to build engaging and informative conversational experiences.

6.1 Designing Engaging Dialog Flows with Claude 3.5

Chatbots are computer programs that simulate conversation with human users through text or voice interactions. They are designed to mimic human conversation and provide a convenient and accessible way for users to interact with a system or service. Here are some key characteristics of chatbots:

Automated Responses: Chatbots can handle routine inquiries and provide pre-programmed responses to frequently asked questions.

Natural Language Processing (NLP) Integration (Advanced Chatbots): Some chatbots utilize NLP techniques to understand the intent and context behind user messages, allowing for more natural and dynamic conversations.

Task Completion: Chatbots can be used to complete specific tasks for users, such as booking appointments, placing orders, or troubleshooting technical issues.

24/7 Availability: Chatbots can provide assistance anytime, regardless of business hours or holidays.

Variety of Applications: Chatbots are used in various applications, including customer service, education, healthcare, and e-commerce.

Overall, chatbots can enhance user experience by providing a convenient, efficient, and sometimes even interactive way to access information or complete tasks.

6.2 Designing Engaging Conversational Experiences with Claude 3.5

Claude 3.5's text generation and manipulation abilities can be harnessed to create chatbots and conversational interfaces that are not only informative but also engaging for users. Here's how to leverage Claude 3.5 to design these experiences:

Crafting Compelling Dialogues:

Claude 3.5 shines in its ability to generate natural language text. Here's how to use the SDK to craft captivating conversation flows for your chatbot: * **Define Conversation Goals and Tone:** Set the direction for your chatbot's interactions. Determine the overall purpose of the conversation (e.g., customer service, information provision) and the desired tone (informative, friendly, humorous). You can incorporate these aspects into prompts for Claude 3.5. * **Prompt Claude 3.5 for Responses:** Provide Claude 3.5 with clear instructions on how you want the chatbot to respond to user input. You can specify different response options based on user queries or conversation stages. For instance, you could have prompts for greetings, answering questions, or providing summaries of information.

Understanding User Intent:

A crucial aspect of engaging conversation is understanding the user's underlying goal or meaning behind their messages. Here's how Claude 3.5 can potentially contribute:

* **Claude 3.5 for Basic Intent Recognition:** While Claude 3.5 might not have built-in NLP capabilities for complex intent recognition, it can be helpful for recognizing basic intents through keyword matching or identifying patterns in user queries. You can structure your prompts and conversation flows to account for these basic intent recognition abilities.
* **Integration with External NLP Tools (if applicable):** Consider integrating Claude 3.5 with a separate Natural Language Processing (NLP) library or tool. This NLP tool can analyze user input for deeper intent recognition, and Claude 3.5 can then leverage the extracted intent to generate more relevant and user-focused responses.

Contextual Awareness for Natural Flow

Conversations become more natural when they acknowledge past interactions. Here's how to use Claude 3.5 to maintain context within your chatbot:

* **Track Conversation History:** Design your system to store and access the conversation history between the user and the chatbot.

```
*    **Prompt    Claude    3.5    with    Context:**
Incorporate  the  conversation  history  or  relevant
parts  of  it  into  your  prompts  for  Claude  3.5.
This  will  allow  Claude  3.5  to  generate  responses
that    consider    the    context    of    previous
interactions,  making  the  conversation  feel  more
natural  and  engaging  for  the  user.
```

By following these guidelines and effectively using Claude 3.5's text generation capabilities, you can design chatbots and conversational interfaces that go beyond simple scripted interactions and provide a more natural and engaging user experience. The next section will delve into how Claude 3.5 can be integrated with existing chatbot frameworks to create robust conversational interfaces.

6.3 Claude 3.5 Integration with Existing Chatbot Frameworks

While Claude 3.5 is a powerful tool for text generation and manipulation, it likely won't function as a standalone chatbot development platform. Here's how Claude 3.5 can be a valuable asset when integrated with existing chatbot frameworks:

API Integration:

Many chatbot frameworks provide APIs (Application Programming Interfaces) that allow you to extend their functionalities by integrating external tools and services. * Explore the possibility of integrating Claude 3.5's SDK with your chosen chatbot framework through its API. This would allow you to leverage Claude 3.5's text generation and manipulation capabilities within your chatbot's conversation flows. * For instance, imagine a scenario where a user interacts with a chatbot requesting a product description. The chatbot framework might handle the core logic of routing the request and identifying the relevant product. However, it could then utilize the Claude 3.5 SDK through the API to dynamically generate a compelling and informative product description tailored to the specific product and user.

Modular Design:

Consider adopting a modular design for your chatbot where Claude 3.5 handles specific tasks within the conversation flow. Here's how this might work: * The core logic and conversation management might be handled by the chatbot framework. It would be responsible for routing user requests, managing conversation flow, and potentially performing actions based on user input. * Claude 3.5, integrated as a separate module, would be called upon for specific functionalities. This could involve tasks like: * Generating creative text formats (e.g., poems, scripts) based on user prompts. * Summarizing factual information retrieved from the chatbot framework. * Paraphrasing user requests or responses to improve clarity or flow of conversation.

By leveraging a modular approach, you can create chatbots that benefit from the strengths of both Claude 3.5 and the chatbot framework you're using. The chatbot framework handles the core conversation mechanics, while Claude 3.5 augments those functionalities with its advanced text generation and manipulation capabilities.

The next section will showcase a concrete example of how Claude 3.5 could be integrated into a restaurant recommendation chatbot to illustrate these concepts in action.

6.4 Example: Building a Restaurant Recommendation Chatbot with Claude 3.5

Here's a simplified example to illustrate how Claude 3.5 could be integrated into a restaurant recommendation chatbot:

Scenario: A user is looking for a restaurant using a chatbot.

Components:

Chatbot Framework: Handles core conversation flow, user interaction, and data retrieval.

Claude 3.5 SDK: Provides text generation and manipulation functionalities.

Conversation Flow:

User Input: The user interacts with the chatbot, expressing their desire to find a restaurant (e.g., "Hi, I'm looking for a restaurant").

Intent Recognition (Chatbot Framework): The chatbot framework analyzes the user's message and identifies the intent (find restaurant).

User Preference Gathering (Chatbot Framework): The chatbot framework might ask the user for their preferences using multiple-choice prompts or open-ended questions (e.g., "What kind of cuisine are you interested in?" or "Do you have a specific price range in mind?"). The chatbot framework would store these preferences for later use.

Claude 3.5 Integration (Chatbot Framework): The chatbot framework interacts with the Claude 3.5 SDK, providing prompts or instructions based on the gathered information.

Prompt 1: "Generate a list of restaurants in [user's location] based on user preferences (cuisine, price range) retrieved earlier."

Claude 3.5 Response (SDK): Claude 3.5 utilizes its knowledge and access to external data sources (potentially integrated by the chatbot framework) to generate a list of restaurants that match the user's preferences.

Chatbot Response (Chatbot Framework): The chatbot framework receives the list of restaurants from Claude 3.5 and presents it to the user in a user-friendly format (e.g., names, descriptions, links).

User Refinement (Optional): The user might choose a restaurant from the list or ask for further options by providing additional preferences. The chatbot framework would handle this and potentially generate new prompts for Claude 3.5 based on the user's refinements.

Further Interaction: The chatbot framework can handle further user requests related to the chosen restaurant (e.g., making a reservation, viewing menus) or provide functionalities for the user to explore other restaurants based on their evolving preferences.

Claude 3.5's Contribution:

In this example, Claude 3.5 doesn't replace the chatbot framework. Instead, it acts as a powerful module within the chatbot, specifically enhancing its restaurant recommendation capabilities by:

Generating dynamic restaurant lists: Claude 3.5 can consider various factors like user preferences, location, and external data sources to create personalized restaurant recommendations.

Enhancing restaurant descriptions: Claude 3.5 can generate concise and engaging descriptions for the recommended restaurants, summarizing key information and potentially adding a touch of creativity.

This is a basic example, but it demonstrates the potential of using Claude 3.5 in conjunction with a chatbot framework to create more informative and engaging conversational interfaces for various applications. The next section will explore some additional considerations and best practices to keep in mind when using Claude 3.5 for chatbot development.

6.5 Additional Considerations and Best Practices for Chatbot Development with Claude 3.5

While Claude 3.5 offers exciting possibilities for chatbot development, here are some additional considerations and best practices to ensure a successful implementation:

Error Handling and Edge Cases:

Design for Unexpected Inputs: Users might provide unexpected questions or requests. Your chatbot should have mechanisms to handle these situations gracefully.

Consider implementing prompts or responses that acknowledge the user's input and offer alternative options or ways to rephrase their request.

You can potentially train Claude 3.5 on a dataset of common user errors or misunderstandings to improve its ability to handle unexpected situations.

Identify Claude 3.5's Limitations: Claude 3.5's responses might not always be perfect. It's crucial to have mechanisms in place to identify and address potential issues with Claude 3.5's generated text.

Integrate quality checks within your chatbot framework to assess the generated responses before presenting them to the user. This might involve checking for factual inconsistencies, inappropriate language, or nonsensical content.

Data Privacy and Security:

User Data Collection: If your chatbot collects user data to personalize interactions or improve recommendations, ensure you have explicit user consent and adhere to data privacy regulations (e.g., GDPR).

Data Security Measures: Implement appropriate security measures to protect user data collected by your chatbot. This might involve encryption of sensitive information and secure storage practices.

Continuous Improvement and User Feedback:

Gather User Feedback: Actively solicit user feedback to identify areas for improvement in your chatbot.

Pay attention to user comments regarding Claude 3.5's generated responses. This feedback can be used to refine prompts for Claude 3.5 or identify areas where Claude 3.5 needs further training data.

Monitor Chatbot Performance: Continuously monitor your chatbot's performance metrics, such as user satisfaction rates, task completion success rates, and the number of errors encountered.

Analyze this data to identify areas where Claude 3.5 can be further integrated or optimized to enhance the overall chatbot experience.

By following these best practices and carefully considering the capabilities and limitations of Claude 3.5, you can leverage its power to create chatbots and conversational interfaces that are informative, engaging, and provide a valuable user experience.

Chapter 7: Enhancing Data Analysis with Claude 3.5

Data analysis is a crucial aspect of various fields, and Claude 3.5 can be a valuable tool to augment your data exploration and analysis workflows. This chapter explores how Claude 3.5 can empower you to gain deeper insights from your data.

7.1 Data Exploration and Visualization with Claude 3.5

Claude 3.5 can be a valuable asset in your data exploration and visualization endeavors. Here's how you can leverage its capabilities to gain deeper understanding from your data:

Uncovering Patterns and Trends

Prompting Claude 3.5 for Insights:

Instead of just relying on statistical analysis, you can utilize Claude 3.5 to identify patterns and trends in a more comprehensive way.

Provide Claude 3.5 with summaries of your data, such as key metrics or descriptive statistics.

Craft prompts that ask Claude 3.5 to analyze the data and highlight important patterns, trends, or relationships between variables. For instance, you could prompt: "Analyze the sales data and identify any correlations between customer demographics and purchase history."

Explaining Insights in Natural Language:

Claude 3.5 excels at generating natural language text. This can be beneficial for understanding complex data patterns.

Once Claude 3.5 identifies patterns, you can prompt it to explain those patterns in clear and concise language. This can help you gain a deeper understanding of the underlying factors driving the observed trends.

Data Visualization Prompts

Generating Custom Visualizations:

Claude 3.5 can be a tool to assist in creating data visualizations. While it might not directly generate charts or graphs itself, it can help you define them.

Craft prompts that describe the data and the desired visualization type. For example: "Generate a scatter plot to visualize the correlation between customer age and purchase amount for electronics."

You can then use these descriptions to create the visualizations in your preferred data analysis tools.

Tailoring Visualizations for Specific Audiences:

Claude 3.5 can help you adapt data visualizations for different audiences.

Provide Claude 3.5 with information about the intended audience (e.g., technical background, decision-makers) and the data you want to convey.

Claude 3.5 can then suggest appropriate visualization types and ways to present the data in a way that resonates with the target audience.

By effectively using Claude 3.5 for these purposes, you can move beyond simply identifying patterns in your data and gain a richer understanding of the underlying stories within your data. The next section explores how Claude 3.5 can be used for data storytelling and generating insights.

7.2 Data Storytelling and Insights Generation with Claude 3.5

Data analysis is not just about crunching numbers; it's about uncovering the narratives hidden within your data. Claude 3.5 can be a powerful tool to transform your data analysis results into compelling stories and generate valuable insights.

Transforming Data into Compelling Narratives

Communicating Findings Through Text:

Data analysis reports can be dense and technical. Claude 3.5 can help translate your findings into clear and concise narratives.

Provide Claude 3.5 with the key takeaways from your analysis, including the most important trends and insights.

You can then prompt Claude 3.5 to generate a data-driven story that highlights the significance of these findings. This can make your analysis more engaging and easier to understand for both technical and non-technical audiences.

Tailoring the Story for Impact:

Claude 3.5 can help craft data stories tailored for specific purposes.

Consider the intended audience and the message you want to convey. You can provide Claude 3.5 with this information alongside your data insights.

Claude 3.5 can then generate a story that emphasizes the aspects most relevant to your audience and drives the desired impact, such as persuading stakeholders or guiding decision-making processes.

Hypothesis Formulation and Exploration

Generating New Ideas from Data:

Claude 3.5 can assist you in going beyond simply reporting what the data says and delve into the "why" behind the observations.

Provide Claude 3.5 with your analysis results and prompt it to suggest potential explanations for the observed trends or patterns.

Claude 3.5 can generate hypotheses based on the data, sparking new ideas for further investigation and potentially leading to new discoveries.

Exploring the Implications of Insights:

Data analysis is not just about the past; it's about informing future actions. Claude 3.5 can help you explore the broader implications of your findings.

Prompt Claude 3.5 to analyze your data insights and suggest potential consequences or areas where these insights might be applicable.

This can help you identify opportunities for improvement, make data-driven predictions, or inform strategic decision-making.

By leveraging Claude 3.5's capabilities for data storytelling and insights generation, you can transform your data analysis from a technical exercise into a strategic tool for driving informed decision-making and achieving your goals. The next section will explore how Claude 3.5 can be used to enhance data cleaning and preprocessing tasks.

7.3 Data Cleaning and Preprocessing with Claude 3.5

Data cleaning and preprocessing are crucial initial steps in any data analysis project. Claude 3.5, with its text generation and manipulation capabilities, can be a valuable asset in this stage. Here's how you can integrate Claude 3.5 into your data cleaning workflow:

Identifying Anomalies and Inconsistencies

Training Claude 3.5 for Anomaly Detection:

You can train Claude 3.5 to identify anomalies within your data by providing it with a set of clean data samples.

Claude 3.5 can learn patterns from this clean data and then analyze new datasets, highlighting potential anomalies or inconsistencies that deviate from the established patterns.

Utilizing Anomaly Reports for Data Correction:

Once Claude 3.5 identifies anomalies, you can investigate them further to determine if they represent errors or actual outliers.

Claude 3.5 can't fix the data itself, but its anomaly reports can significantly reduce the time and effort required to pinpoint data quality issues within your dataset.

Text Summarization for Large Text Datasets

Claude 3.5 for Textual Data Processing:

Data cleaning often involves handling textual data. Claude 3.5 can be a powerful tool for processing large volumes of text.

If your dataset includes textual elements like customer reviews, social media posts, or survey responses, Claude 3.5 can help you summarize and analyze this data efficiently.

Identifying Themes and Sentiment:

Claude 3.5's summarization capabilities can help you identify key themes or sentiment within your textual data.

While Claude 3.5 might not have built-in sentiment analysis, you can potentially use it alongside sentiment analysis tools.

Claude 3.5 can summarize the textual data, and the sentiment analysis tool can categorize the sentiment (positive, negative, neutral) of the summarized text.

This can provide valuable insights into customer opinions, social media trends, or overall user sentiment within your data.

Integration with Data Cleaning Tools

Claude 3.5 is unlikely to function as a standalone data cleaning platform. Here's how it can collaborate with other tools:

Data Cleaning Pipeline with Python Libraries:

Imagine a scenario where you use Python libraries like Pandas for initial data cleaning tasks (handling missing values, identifying duplicates).

You can then utilize Claude 3.5's anomaly detection capabilities within your Python code to identify more complex data quality issues that Pandas might miss.

Interactive Data Cleaning with Jupyter Notebooks:

Jupyter Notebooks provide an interactive environment for data analysis.

You can integrate Claude 3.5 with your Jupyter Notebook workflows. This allows you to explore your data, identify potential issues using Claude 3.5's functionalities, and iteratively clean your data in a seamless manner.

By incorporating Claude 3.5 into your data cleaning process, you can automate some tasks, identify data quality issues more effectively, and ultimately prepare your data for robust and reliable analysis. The next section will discuss how Claude 3.5 can be integrated with data analysis tools to create a more comprehensive workflow.

7.4 Integration with Data Analysis Tools

While Claude 3.5 offers a powerful set of functionalities for data analysis, it likely won't function as a standalone platform. Here's how Claude 3.5 can be a valuable asset when integrated with existing data analysis tools:

Enhancing Workflows with Python Libraries

Leveraging Claude 3.5's SDK within Python Code:

Utilize Python libraries like Pandas for data cleaning and preprocessing tasks (handling missing values, identifying outliers).

Integrate Claude 3.5's functionalities into your Python code through the SDK. This allows you to exploit Claude 3.5's capabilities for tasks like:

Anomaly detection (complementing Pandas' functionality)

Text Summarization (analyzing large datasets of reviews, social media posts)

Hypothesis generation (prompting Claude 3.5 to analyze trends and suggest explanations)

Utilize data visualization libraries like Matplotlib or Seaborn to create charts and graphs based on your analysis and Claude 3.5's insights.

Interactive Analysis with Dash or Shiny

Data Cleaning and Feature Engineering in Separate Tools:

Clean and prepare your data using familiar data analysis tools like Pandas or R.

Utilize feature engineering techniques to create new variables that might be more insightful for analysis.

Interactive Dashboards with Claude 3.5 Integration:

Integrate Claude 3.5's text generation and analysis functionalities into your interactive dashboards built with tools like Dash or Shiny. This allows users to interact with the data and receive insights generated by Claude 3.5 in real-time. Here's a potential workflow:

Users upload their data to the dashboard.

The dashboard utilizes Pandas or R for data cleaning and feature engineering.

The cleaned data is then fed into Claude 3.5 through the API.

Claude 3.5 generates insights, summaries, or suggested visualizations based on the data and user prompts within the dashboard.

The dashboard displays the data, visualizations, and Claude 3.5's insights in an interactive format, allowing users to explore the data further and gain a deeper understanding.

By combining Claude 3.5 with existing data analysis tools, you can create more comprehensive and interactive data exploration and analysis workflows. The next section will showcase a concrete example of how Claude 3.5 can be used to analyze customer reviews, demonstrating its practical applications within data analysis.

7.5 Case Study: Analyzing Customer Reviews with Claude 3.5

Let's revisit the scenario of analyzing customer reviews for your e-commerce store to illustrate how Claude 3.5 can be applied in a practical data analysis setting.

Data Source: Imagine you have a dataset of customer reviews for various products on your online store.

Workflow with Claude 3.5 Integration:

Data Cleaning and Preprocessing:

Use Python libraries like Pandas to clean the data (handling missing values, removing irrelevant information).

Text Summarization and Sentiment Analysis (if applicable):

Utilize Claude 3.5 to summarize the reviews for each product, highlighting key themes and recurring points mentioned by customers.

If sentiment analysis is not built into Claude 3.5, consider integrating a sentiment analysis tool. This tool can categorize each review (positive, negative, neutral) and provide an overall sentiment score for each product.

Identifying Trends and Insights with Claude 3.5:

Prompt Claude 3.5 to analyze the summarized reviews and sentiment analysis results (if applicable).

Ask Claude 3.5 to identify:

Common praises and criticisms mentioned in the reviews.

Products with consistently positive or negative sentiment.

Potential correlations between sentiment and product features mentioned in the reviews (e.g., negative sentiment related to product durability).

Actionable Insights and Data Visualization:

Based on the insights from Claude 3.5 and sentiment analysis (if applicable), you can:

Identify areas for product improvement based on negative feedback.

Highlight positive aspects consistently mentioned in reviews for marketing purposes.

Create charts or graphs (using libraries like Matplotlib) to visualize sentiment distribution across different product categories or price ranges.

Benefits of Claude 3.5 Integration:

Efficiency: Claude 3.5 can automate text summarization, saving you time compared to manually reading through all reviews.

Identifying Hidden Patterns: Claude 3.5 can potentially identify subtle patterns within the reviews that you might miss through manual analysis.

Actionable Insights: The combination of Claude 3.5's analysis and sentiment analysis (if applicable) can provide valuable customer feedback that can be used to improve products and marketing strategies.

This case study demonstrates how Claude 3.5 can be a valuable tool within your data analysis workflows, particularly when dealing with textual data like customer reviews. By combining its capabilities with existing data analysis tools, you can gain deeper customer insights and make data-driven decisions to improve your business.

Chapter 8: Visualizing Data with Claude 3.5's Artifacts Feature

Data visualization is a crucial aspect of data analysis. It allows you to communicate complex information in a clear and understandable way. Claude 3.5's Artifacts feature introduces exciting possibilities for data visualization, transforming static charts and graphs into interactive elements within your workflow.

8.1 Beyond Static Visualizations: Interactive Insights with Claude 3.5 Artifacts

Traditionally, data visualization tools like Matplotlib or Seaborn generate static charts and graphs. Claude 3.5's Artifacts feature breaks this mold by introducing the possibility of **interactive visualizations**, transforming data exploration and communication.

Unlocking Interactivity with Artifacts

Interactive Elements within Visualizations: Imagine a scatter plot created by Claude 3.5's Artifact that visualizes the correlation between customer age and purchase amount. This wouldn't be a static image. Users could:

Hover over data points: Reveal additional information about specific customers (e.g., purchase history, location).

Filter the data: Focus on specific age groups or purchase ranges to explore trends in more detail.

Dynamic Data Updates: Claude 3.5 Artifacts can potentially **update visualizations in real-time** as new data becomes available. This is beneficial for:

Monitoring social media sentiment: An Artifact could display a live-updating chart showing how brand sentiment changes on Twitter over time.

Tracking website traffic: An interactive visualization could track user behavior and website performance in real-time.

These interactive features go beyond static visualizations, allowing users to engage with the data more deeply and gain richer insights.

8.2 Workflows for Interactive Data Visualization with Claude 3.5 Artifacts

While Claude 3.5's Artifacts feature offers exciting possibilities for interactive data visualization, it likely won't replace your existing tools entirely. Here's how to create a workflow that leverages the strengths of both:

1. Utilize Existing Data Visualization Tools:

Begin by using your preferred data analysis tools (e.g., Python libraries like Matplotlib or Seaborn) to generate the core visualizations based on your data.

These tools provide a strong foundation for creating clear and informative visualizations.

2. Export for Use with Claude 3.5 Artifacts:

There are two ways to provide Claude 3.5 with the data for your interactive visualizations:

Export the visualizations themselves: If your data visualization tools allow it, export the charts or graphs you created in a format compatible with Claude 3.5's Artifacts feature.

Provide detailed descriptions: If exporting visualizations isn't possible, create detailed descriptions of the desired visualizations. This should include the data you want to represent, the visualization type (scatter plot, bar chart, etc.), and any labels or axes required.

3. Prompt Claude 3.5 for Interactive Elements:

Once you have your exported visualizations or detailed descriptions, provide them to Claude 3.5.

Instruct Claude 3.5 to use its Artifacts feature to transform these static elements into interactive visualizations.

Be specific about the desired interactivity. Here are some examples:

Hover-over information: Instruct Claude 3.5 to display additional details (e.g., data point specifics) when a user hovers over a specific element within the visualization.

Data filtering: Allow users to filter the data based on certain criteria (e.g., product category, date range) by incorporating interactive filters within the Artifact.

4. Integrate into Your Workflow:

Consider how these interactive Claude 3.5 Artifacts fit within your existing data analysis workflows.

Explore how to seamlessly integrate Claude 3.5's functionalities with your preferred data analysis tools. This might involve:

Utilizing Python code to connect Claude 3.5's API to your data analysis environment.

Using web development frameworks to integrate Claude 3.5 Artifacts into dashboards or reports.

By following these steps, you can create a workflow that combines the strengths of traditional data visualization tools with the interactivity offered by Claude 3.5 Artifacts. This can lead to more engaging data exploration and communication experiences.

The next section will explore some compelling use cases for interactive data visualizations.

8.3 Use Cases for Interactive Data Visualizations with Claude 3.5 Artifacts

Claude 3.5 Artifacts' interactive data visualizations open doors to various applications in data exploration, communication, and storytelling. Here are a few examples:

Enhanced Data Exploration for Analysts:

Interactive visualizations empower data analysts to delve deeper into their data.

Imagine a scatter plot visualizing customer purchase history alongside demographics. With hover-over features enabled by Claude 3.5 Artifacts, analysts can explore data point details (e.g., individual customer purchase behavior) to identify patterns or test hypotheses. This interactivity can significantly enhance the data exploration process.

Data Communication and Storytelling:

Static visualizations can be informative, but they can also be passive experiences for audiences.

Interactive visualizations created with Claude 3.5 Artifacts can transform data communication and storytelling.

Imagine a report on social media sentiment analysis that incorporates an interactive Artifact. Viewers can explore sentiment trends over time, filter by specific keywords or demographics, and gain a richer understanding of the data compared to a static report.

Data-Driven Decision Making:

Interactive visualizations can be instrumental in data-driven decision making.

Imagine a sales dashboard that includes an interactive Claude 3.5 Artifact visualizing sales performance across different regions. Sales managers can interact with the visualization to explore trends, identify underperforming regions, and make informed decisions about resource allocation or marketing strategies.

Educational Tools and Simulations:

Claude 3.5 Artifacts can be incorporated into educational tools and simulations.

Imagine a science simulation where students can interact with a Claude 3.5 Artifact to visualize the effects of changing variables in an experiment. This interactivity can enhance student engagement and understanding of complex scientific concepts.

These are just a few examples, and the possibilities are vast. By leveraging Claude 3.5 Artifacts' interactive features, you can create more engaging and impactful data visualizations that cater to various purposes.

The next section will address some important considerations and best practices to keep in mind when working with Claude 3.5 Artifacts.

8.4 Considerations and Best Practices for Interactive Data Visualizations with Claude 3.5 Artifacts

While Claude 3.5 Artifacts offer exciting possibilities for interactive data visualization, it's important to approach them with a thoughtful strategy. Here are some key considerations and best practices:

Balancing Interactivity with Clarity:

Prioritize User Experience: While interactivity is valuable, avoid overwhelming users with excessive features. Ensure the core message of the data visualization remains clear and easy to understand.

Test and Refine: Once you create an interactive visualization, test it with users to identify any confusing elements or functionalities. Gather feedback and refine the Artifact to optimize the user experience.

Data Volume and Performance:

Consider Data Complexity: Claude 3.5 Artifacts might not be ideal for visualizing extremely large or complex datasets. Complex visualizations with a high number of data points could lead to performance issues.

Optimize for Performance: If dealing with large datasets, explore ways to simplify the visualization or break it down into smaller, more manageable components within the Artifact.

Accessibility and Usability:

Ensure Accessibility: Strive to create interactive visualizations that are accessible to users with disabilities. This might involve providing alternative text descriptions for visual elements or ensuring keyboard navigation compatibility.

Usability Testing: Similar to testing for clarity, conduct usability tests to identify any accessibility barriers or confusing functionalities within your Claude 3.5 Artifacts.

Integration and Workflow Management:

Choose Appropriate Integration Methods: The best method for integrating Claude 3.5 Artifacts with your workflow depends on your technical expertise and project requirements.

Consider Python code for programmatic control within your data analysis environment.

Explore web development frameworks for seamless integration into dashboards or reports.

Maintain Clear Documentation: If your project involves multiple team members, document the process of creating and integrating Claude 3.5 Artifacts. This ensures clarity and consistency throughout the workflow.

By following these best practices and carefully considering the limitations of Claude 3.5 Artifacts, you can leverage their interactive capabilities to create impactful data visualizations that enhance your data exploration, communication, and decision-making efforts.

Chapter 9: Exploring Advanced Applications of Claude 3.5

Claude 3.5, with its advanced capabilities in reasoning, code generation, and visual analysis, opens doors to various exciting applications beyond data exploration and visualization. This chapter delves into some of these advanced use cases:

9.1 Automating Repetitive Tasks with Claude 3.5

Claude 3.5's potential for automating repetitive tasks can significantly improve your efficiency in data analysis workflows. Here are two areas where Claude 3.5 can be particularly helpful:

Code Generation for Data Analysis:

Imagine this scenario: You need to calculate descriptive statistics (e.g., mean, median, standard deviation) for several variables across multiple datasets. Traditionally, you might write repetitive Python code using libraries like Pandas for each dataset.

Claude 3.5 to the rescue: Provide Claude 3.5 with a high-level description of the task, like "calculate descriptive statistics for all numerical variables in each CSV file within this folder." Claude 3.5, with its understanding of data analysis and Python code generation, could potentially create a script that automates this process.

This would significantly reduce the time and effort required for such tasks, especially when dealing with numerous datasets.

Data Cleaning and Preprocessing Automation:

Data cleaning and preprocessing often involve repetitive tasks like identifying and fixing missing values, formatting inconsistencies, or converting data types. Claude 3.5 can learn from examples and automate some of these steps.

Here's an example: You provide Claude 3.5 with a clean dataset and its corresponding unclean version. You instruct Claude 3.5 to analyze the differences and identify patterns in errors or inconsistencies.

Based on this analysis, Claude 3.5 could potentially generate Python code to address these specific data cleaning steps. This code could then be applied to similar datasets in the future, saving you time and ensuring consistency in your data cleaning process.

Important Considerations:

Claude 3.5 is unlikely to write perfect code in every instance, and it might require human intervention or refinement.

The effectiveness of Claude 3.5's automation capabilities depends on the complexity of the tasks. It might struggle with highly specialized data analysis or cleaning procedures.

However, Claude 3.5's potential to automate repetitive tasks can be a valuable asset in your data analysis toolkit, freeing you up for more strategic tasks and complex problem-solving.

9.2 Enhancing Scientific Discovery with Claude 3.5

Claude 3.5's ability to process and analyze information can be a powerful tool in scientific discovery. Here are two ways Claude 3.5 can augment the scientific research process:

Hypothesis Generation and Exploration:

Scientific discovery often involves a crucial step: formulating hypotheses that can be tested through experimentation. Claude 3.5 can be a valuable partner in this phase.

Imagine a scenario: You're a researcher studying the effects of a new fertilizer on crop yield. You have a dataset containing historical data on crop yields, weather patterns, and fertilizer application.

Claude 3.5 can assist you by:

Analyzing the data to identify potential correlations between crop yield and various factors like fertilizer application rates or weather conditions.

Based on these correlations, Claude 3.5 can suggest potential hypotheses. For instance, it might suggest a hypothesis that "increasing fertilizer application rates within a specific range leads to higher crop yields."

These hypotheses can then be further investigated through controlled experiments to validate or disprove them. Claude 3.5 can thus spark new ideas and guide researchers towards promising avenues for scientific inquiry.

Simulating Complex Systems:

Scientific research often involves studying complex systems, such as weather patterns, disease outbreaks, or economic models. Claude 3.5's capabilities can be beneficial for simulating the behavior of these systems.

For example: You're researching the spread of a contagious disease. You have data on historical infection rates, population demographics, and travel patterns.

Claude 3.5 can be used to:

Analyze the data to understand the factors influencing disease transmission.

Based on this analysis, Claude 3.5 could create a simulation model that mimics the spread of the disease under different conditions. This could allow researchers to test the effectiveness of various intervention strategies (e.g., vaccination campaigns) within the simulated environment.

Claude 3.5's simulation capabilities can be a valuable tool for understanding complex systems and predicting their behavior under different scenarios.

Important Considerations:

Claude 3.5's scientific understanding is based on the data it is trained on. It's crucial to ensure the quality and relevance of the data used for training Claude 3.5 in a scientific context.

Scientific hypotheses generated by Claude 3.5 need to be rigorously tested through experimentation. Claude 3.5 should not replace the scientific method but rather augment it.

By leveraging Claude 3.5's capabilities for hypothesis generation and complex system simulation, researchers can advance scientific discovery and make significant contributions to various fields.

9.3 Augmenting Creative Processes with Claude 3.5

Claude 3.5's ability to understand and generate creative text formats can be a valuable asset for various creative endeavors. Here are two potential applications:

Storytelling and Content Creation:

Writers often experience writer's block or struggle to develop ideas further. Claude 3.5 can provide assistance throughout the creative writing process.

Scenario: You're a novelist working on a science fiction story. You have a basic plot outline but are stuck on developing a specific scene.

Claude 3.5 can help you by:

Expanding on your ideas: Provide Claude 3.5 with your plot outline and instruct it to generate creative text formats that elaborate on a specific scene. It could generate a dialogue between characters, a description of the setting, or even a poem that captures the mood of the scene.

Generating different creative text formats: If you're unsure of the direction you want to take your story, Claude 3.5 can provide options. Instruct it to generate a scene in the form of a news report, a diary entry, or a screenplay, giving you fresh perspectives on how to approach the narrative.

By providing prompts and direction, Claude 3.5 can spark creativity, overcome writer's block, and offer new avenues for storytelling.

Concept Art and Design Exploration:

The initial stages of creative design projects often involve brainstorming and sketching ideas. Claude 3.5 can add to this process by generating visual concepts based on your text descriptions.

Imagine you're a graphic designer working on a new logo for a tech company. You have a concept in mind, but you need some visual inspiration to get started.

Claude 3.5 can assist you by:

Translating your ideas into visual concepts: Describe your concept to Claude 3.5 in detail, including the desired style, colors, and mood. Claude 3.5 could then generate prototype images that visually represent your design ideas.

Exploring variations on a theme: Provide Claude 3.5 with a basic concept and instruct it to generate variations on that theme. This could involve different color palettes, layouts, or stylistic elements, giving you a broader range of design options to consider.

Claude 3.5 can be a valuable tool for visualizing design concepts and exploring creative possibilities in the initial stages of a project.

Important Considerations:

Claude 3.5's creative outputs are based on the data and text it has been trained on. It may not always align perfectly with your unique creative vision.

The quality of the prompts and instructions you provide to Claude 3.5 significantly impacts the quality of the generated creative text formats or images.

By using Claude 3.5 as a collaborator rather than a replacement for human creativity, you can leverage its capabilities to enhance your storytelling, content creation, and design exploration processes.

9.4 Important Considerations and Ethical Implications of Claude 3.5

Claude 3.5's potential to automate tasks, generate creative text formats, and analyze information is impressive. However, it's crucial to approach this powerful tool with a critical eye and consider the following ethical implications:

Bias and Fairness in AI-Generated Outputs:

Large language models like Claude 3.5 are trained on massive amounts of text data. This data can contain biases and stereotypes that reflect the real world. Consequently, the outputs generated by Claude 3.5, whether code, creative text formats, or data analysis results, may also reflect these biases.

Mitigation Strategies:

Be aware of potential biases in Claude 3.5's training data and how they might influence its outputs.

Carefully evaluate the outputs generated by Claude 3.5 for signs of bias. Consider using Claude 3.5's outputs as a starting point and exercising human judgment to identify and mitigate any biases before implementation.

Advocate for Claude 3.5 to be trained on more diverse and inclusive datasets to minimize bias in future iterations of the model.

Human Oversight and Control:

Claude 3.5 is a powerful tool, but it shouldn't replace human judgment or expertise. Claude 3.5's reasoning processes are complex, and it may not always be clear how it arrives at its outputs.

Maintaining Control:

Always critically evaluate the outputs generated by Claude 3.5. Ensure they align with your goals, requirements, and ethical principles.

Do not rely solely on Claude 3.5 for decision-making. Use human expertise to interpret Claude 3.5's outputs and make informed decisions.

Additional Considerations:

Transparency and Explainability: As AI models become more complex, ensuring transparency in their reasoning processes is crucial. Future advancements in Claude 3.5 might involve improved capabilities to explain the rationale behind its generated code, data analysis results, or creative outputs.

Accountability: The development and deployment of AI models involve ethical considerations. There needs to be a clear understanding of who is accountable for the outputs generated by Claude 3.5, especially if they have negative consequences.

By carefully considering these ethical implications and maintaining human oversight, Claude 3.5 can be a powerful tool for good. Responsible development and use of AI are essential to ensure Claude 3.5 contributes to a positive and equitable future.

9.5 The Future of Claude 3.5 and Advanced Applications

Claude 3.5 is a rapidly evolving large language model, and its capabilities are constantly being improved by Anthropic. As Claude 3.5 continues to develop, we can expect even more advanced applications to emerge in various fields. Here are some potential future directions:

Integration with Specialized Software:

Imagine a future where Claude 3.5 seamlessly integrates with specialized software programs used in specific domains. For example:

Scientific research: Claude 3.5 could be integrated with software used for data analysis in biology, chemistry, or physics. This could allow scientists to leverage Claude 3.5's capabilities for hypothesis generation, data exploration, and simulation directly within their familiar workflow.

Engineering design: Claude 3.5 could be integrated with engineering software used for computer-aided design (CAD) or finite element analysis (FEA). This could enable engineers to utilize Claude 3.5 for tasks like concept generation, material selection, or structural analysis, all within their design environment.

Creative design applications: Integration with creative design software could allow graphic designers, product designers, or architects to use Claude 3.5 for tasks like generating design variations, creating mood boards, or suggesting color palettes.

Such integration would bridge the gap between Claude 3.5's general-purpose AI capabilities and the specialized functionalities of domain-specific software. This could lead to significant advancements in various fields by empowering professionals with a powerful AI assistant tailored to their specific needs.

Explainability and Transparency in AI Reasoning:

As AI models become more complex, ensuring explainability and transparency in their reasoning processes becomes crucial. Anthropic is likely to prioritize advancements in this area for Claude 3.5.

Future iterations of Claude 3.5 might be able to explain their reasoning behind:

Generated code: Claude 3.5 could explain the thought process behind the code it generates for data analysis tasks, making it easier for users to understand and adapt the code if needed.

Data insights: When presenting data analysis results, Claude 3.5 could explain the key factors or patterns it identified within the data to support its insights.

Creative outputs: In the context of creative writing or concept art generation, Claude 3.5 could explain the rationale behind its suggestions, allowing users to understand the thought process behind the creative text formats or images generated.

This improved explainability would increase trust and user confidence in Claude 3.5's capabilities, fostering wider adoption and responsible use of the technology.

The potential applications of Claude 3.5 are vast and constantly evolving. By leveraging its capabilities for automation, analysis, and creative exploration, Claude 3.5 has the potential to play a significant role in shaping the future of various industries and disciplines. However, it's important to remember that AI is a tool, and its impact depends on the way we develop and use it. Responsible development and ethical considerations are paramount to ensure Claude 3.5 contributes to a positive and equitable future.

Chapter 10: A Glimpse into the Future of AI with Claude and Beyond

Claude 3.5 represents a significant leap forward in large language model (LLM) technology. Its capabilities for reasoning, code generation, and data analysis open doors to a future brimming with possibilities. This chapter explores some potential future directions for AI, building upon the foundation laid by Claude 3.5:

10.1 Beyond Human-Level Performance: AI Specialization and Collaboration

Claude 3.5 showcases the impressive capabilities of large language models (LLMs). However, it's important to consider the future of AI beyond achieving human-level performance across all tasks. A more promising approach might lie in specialization and collaboration.

Imagine a future with AI models specifically designed for various domains:

Medical Diagnosis: An AI trained on vast medical datasets and equipped with reasoning abilities could assist doctors in analyzing complex medical cases, identifying potential diagnoses, and suggesting treatment plans.

Legal Research: AI متخصص (mutakhasiss - Arabic for "specialized") in legal research could analyze legal documents, case law, and regulations to identify relevant precedents and support legal arguments.

Software Development: AI specializing in code generation could translate natural language requirements into efficient code, automate repetitive coding tasks, and identify potential bugs or security vulnerabilities.

These specialized AI models would not necessarily need to outperform humans in every aspect. Instead, their deep understanding of their specific domains would make them invaluable collaborators alongside human experts.

Human-AI collaboration is likely to be a defining feature of the future:

Humans bring domain knowledge, intuition, ethical considerations, and the ability to adapt to unforeseen situations.

AI excels at handling vast amounts of data, identifying patterns, and automating tasks with high accuracy and speed.

This powerful partnership between humans and specialized AI has the potential to revolutionize various fields and lead to significant breakthroughs.

Here are some potential benefits of human-AI collaboration:

Improved decision-making: By combining human judgment with AI-powered data analysis, complex decisions can be made with greater accuracy and efficiency.

Enhanced creativity and innovation: AI can assist humans in exploring new ideas, generating creative text formats, and identifying hidden patterns within data, fostering innovation across various disciplines.

Increased productivity and efficiency: AI can automate repetitive tasks, freeing up human experts to focus on higher-level cognitive tasks and strategic problem-solving.

The future of AI is not simply about replicating human intelligence, but rather about creating a powerful synergy between human and artificial intelligence. By leveraging the complementary strengths of both, we can unlock a future filled with possibilities.

10.2 The Rise of AI Assistants and Companions

AI assistants like Claude 3.5 have the potential to evolve into more comprehensive AI companions, fundamentally changing how we interact with technology and navigate our daily lives.

Imagine a future with personalized AI companions that:

Learn your preferences and anticipate your needs: Your AI companion could understand your habits, routines, and goals. It could proactively suggest tasks, manage your schedule, and provide reminders based on your preferences.

Assist you with various tasks: From scheduling appointments and managing your to-do list to controlling your smart home devices and streamlining online tasks, your AI companion could be your digital butler, freeing you up for more important matters.

Provide personalized education and entertainment: Your AI companion could curate educational content tailored to your interests and learning style. It could also recommend books, movies, or music based on your preferences, offering a personalized entertainment experience.

However, the development of AI companions raises important ethical considerations:

Privacy and Security: As AI companions become more integrated into our lives, safeguarding personal data becomes crucial. Robust security measures and clear guidelines regarding data collection and usage are essential.

Bias and Fairness: AI companions inherit biases from the data they are trained on. It's important to ensure these companions are fair and unbiased in their interactions and recommendations.

Human Connection and Emotional Dependence: Overreliance on AI companions for social interaction could lead to feelings of isolation. It's important to strike a balance between leveraging AI assistance and maintaining meaningful human connections.

Here are some ways to ensure the responsible development of AI companions:

Transparency and User Control: Users should have clear control over the data collected by their AI companions and how it's used. Additionally, companions should be transparent about their limitations and reasoning processes.

Human-in-the-Loop Design: AI companions should be designed to complement human interaction, not replace it. Humans should always be in control and have the ability to override AI suggestions or recommendations.

Focus on Empathy and Emotional Intelligence: Future AI companions should be equipped with emotional intelligence to understand and respond to human emotions appropriately. This can foster trust and create a more positive user experience.

By addressing these challenges and prioritizing responsible development, AI companions have the potential to become valuable tools for improving our productivity, well-being, and overall quality of life.

10.3 AI for Social Good: Addressing Global Challenges with Claude 3.5 and Beyond

Claude 3.5's capabilities demonstrate the immense potential of AI to address complex global challenges and contribute to a more sustainable and equitable future. Here, we explore how AI can be harnessed for social good in various areas:

1. Climate Change:

Climate Data Analysis: AI can analyze vast amounts of climate data to understand weather patterns, predict extreme weather events, and assess the impact of climate change on different regions.

Sustainable Energy Solutions: AI can be used to optimize energy production from renewable sources like solar and wind power, identify areas for energy efficiency improvements, and develop smarter energy grids.

Resource Management: AI can help us manage natural resources more effectively, such as optimizing water usage in agriculture or identifying sustainable fishing practices to preserve marine ecosystems.

2. Global Health Initiatives:

Disease Surveillance and Outbreak Prediction: AI can analyze data on disease outbreaks to identify patterns and predict potential epidemics. This allows for early intervention and resource allocation to mitigate the spread of diseases.

Drug Discovery and Personalized Medicine: AI can analyze vast datasets of genetic information and medical records to accelerate drug discovery and development. Additionally, AI can assist in personalized medicine by tailoring treatment plans to individual patients based on their unique genetic makeup and medical history.

Improving Healthcare Accessibility: AI-powered chatbots and virtual assistants can provide basic healthcare information and answer common questions, particularly in underserved areas with limited access to medical professionals.

3. Education and Literacy:

Personalized Learning Experiences: AI tutors can personalize learning experiences for students, catering to their individual needs and learning styles. This can improve educational outcomes and address learning gaps.

Language Learning Tools: AI-powered language learning applications can provide interactive and personalized instruction, making language learning more accessible and efficient for people of all ages.

Bridging the Literacy Gap: AI can be used to develop educational tools that help people overcome illiteracy and improve their reading and writing skills.

4. Other Areas:

AI has the potential to make significant contributions in various other areas, such as:

Disaster Management: AI can be used to analyze real-time data during natural disasters to predict flood zones, optimize rescue efforts, and coordinate emergency response.

Poverty Reduction: AI can be used to identify individuals and communities most affected by poverty and develop targeted programs for social welfare and economic opportunities.

Infrastructure Development: AI can be used to optimize infrastructure planning, predict maintenance needs for bridges and roads, and improve overall infrastructure efficiency.

The key to maximizing AI's positive impact lies in responsible development and implementation. Here are some crucial considerations:

Focus on Equity and Inclusion: AI solutions should be designed to benefit everyone, not exacerbate existing inequalities.

Collaboration between Stakeholders: Governments, businesses, NGOs, and research institutions need to collaborate to ensure AI is used ethically and effectively for social good.

Continuous Monitoring and Evaluation: The impact of AI initiatives needs to be monitored and evaluated to ensure they are achieving their goals and not causing unintended consequences.

By leveraging AI responsibly and creatively, we can address some of the world's most pressing challenges and create a brighter future for all. Claude 3.5 represents a significant step in this direction, paving the way for a new era of AI-driven solutions for global challenges.

10.4 The Road Ahead: Responsible AI Development and Human-Centered Design

As AI continues to evolve at an unprecedented pace, it's critical to prioritize responsible development and human-centered design principles. This ensures AI is developed and used in a way that benefits humanity and avoids potential pitfalls. Here are some key areas to focus on:

Transparency and Explainability:

AI systems should be transparent in their decision-making processes. Users should be able to understand how AI arrives at its conclusions, especially in high-stakes situations. This fosters trust and allows for human oversight.

Explainable AI (XAI) techniques can help make AI reasoning more understandable. These techniques can explain the factors influencing an AI's decision and how different data points contribute to the final outcome.

Addressing Bias and Fairness:

AI models can perpetuate societal biases if trained on biased data. It's crucial to develop methods to mitigate bias throughout the AI development lifecycle.

Data collection practices need to be scrutinized to ensure datasets used to train AI models are diverse and representative of the real world.

Fairness metrics should be incorporated into AI development to measure potential biases and ensure AI outputs are fair and non-discriminatory.

Human Control and Oversight:

AI should be a tool to augment human capabilities, not replace them. Humans should always maintain control over AI systems and be accountable for their development and deployment.

Guardrails and regulations may be necessary to ensure AI is used safely and ethically in certain sectors, such as healthcare or finance.

Human-in-the-loop (HITL) systems can be designed where a human makes the final decision after considering the recommendations or outputs provided by the AI.

Human-Centered Design:

AI systems should be designed with human needs and values in mind. User-centered design principles should be applied throughout the development process.

User testing and feedback are crucial to ensure AI systems are usable, reliable, and meet the needs of the people who will be using them.

Considering the social and ethical implications of AI systems throughout the design process is essential to avoid unintended consequences.

By adhering to these principles, we can ensure that AI development is responsible and ethical. This will allow AI to reach its full potential as a tool for positive change and progress, benefiting society as a whole.

Remember, AI is a powerful tool. The future of AI depends on the choices we make today. By prioritizing responsible development and human-centered design, we can ensure AI is a force for good in the world.